the matchstick litanies

the matchstick litanies

jo reyes-boitel

Published by
Next Page Press
San Antonio, Texas
www.nextpage-press.com
© 2023 jo reyes-boitel. All rights reserved.

No part of this book may be used or reproduced in any manner without written permission from the publisher, except in context of reviews.

ISBN: 978-1-7366721-4-3
Library of Congress Control Number: 2023940384

Book team:
Laura Van Prooyen, Director and Editor
Cathlin Noonan, Associate Editor
Eileen Curtright, Copy Editor
Josie Prock, Proofreader
Amber Morena, Book Design

Cover photo: jo reyes-boitel
Cover image: Kaylee Hernandez, kayleescameos.com

I wrote this book for the twelve-year-old girl I was.

life
now halted. more and more water add-
itive. the dream less clear. the soil more distant
its prayer of table. bless of lips. more hard to reach w/ penn-

ies. the knife
that should have cut it. the hands that should have
　　—KAMAU BRATHWAITE

Someone I loved once gave me a box full of darkness.
It took me years to understand that this too, was a gift.
　　—MARY OLIVER

Because I have no choice.
　　—GLORIA ANZALDÚA

Contents

the house next door is in flames | one   *1*
   remembrance day   *3*
   half sun   *4*
   date night   *6*
   corner house   *7*
   anthropology   *8*
   house fire   *11*
   bird calls   *13*
   epicenter : 12   *16*
   sleep   *18*
   fisheyes   *19*
   effects   *20*

the house next door is in flames | two   *21*
   epicenter : 9   *22*
   sunday afternoon   *24*
   coupled   *25*
   La Vernia, TX   *26*
   pilgrimage   *27*
   hibiscus   *28*
   what my father buries   *29*
   my mother is the center of this house   *30*
   bitter oranges   *31*

the house next door is in flames | three   *34*
   epicenter : 14   *35*
   echoes   *37*
   poker face   *38*
   bearing gifts   *39*

grandmother mouth   *41*
starless   *42*
record player   *44*
safe house   *45*
ode to the broken clavicle   *46*
my father calls to me   *47*
bruising   *49*
here is what I've learned   *51*
friendly fire   *52*

the house next door is in flames | four   *56*
flint   *57*
amendment   *58*
tinderbox   *59*
slicing fruit   *60*
collateral damage   *61*
staring contest   *62*
my brother the pragmatist   *63*
blasphemy   *64*
familiar   *65*
anticipation   *69*
unmasking   *70*

Acknowledgements   *73*
About the Author   *75*

the matchstick litanies

the house next door is in flames | one

        my body opens like a starfish

      thick-skinned   fevered nodes

          naked, humid   terrible night

pounding   pounding   across the sky
      fireworks in every color
                    just shy of New Year's Eve

2 a.m.   warmth builds up in the living room
windows lit like stained glass at midday, orange and
yellow, creamy through pale curtains and blinds
just before my mother's tender voice calls
me from the open bedroom door just before
someone bangs on the kitchen door again and again
again, the house shaking and before that a sleep deep—
muscles, soft-draped shoulders, head cradled
in pillows—before the too-lit window, diffused
in orange, before crackling wood, the

splintering
jostling my dreaming
mind

sharp notes across a sky
almost green in its darkness
green to umber to blue black

from the sky to the branches
winterbare and fruitless
pecan trees

then the thing itself:

orange and pink
and specks of blue

the frame of a house
inhaling   the walls ballooning
then exhaling   stiffening toward coal

remembrance day

Today is my father's birthday.
He sits at the kitchen table and waits
for my mother to make his birthday eggs
—sunny side up, green chile, and instant coffee.

   He waits
for my phone call and some happy memory,
for my brother to visit with a smile and a six-pack,
for the last of winter to usher itself into the kitchen.

half sun

My feet nestled into my father's shoes.
Shoulders against the closet's back wall,
a drape of button-down shirts
hung in front of me. My feet swam
in his perfect Stacey Adams. I was hiding
but
    my giggle gave me away

    and my father mock-shouted
to convince me he was scared.

I was born hip to hip with my father:
our hands in the truck engine, checking fluids,
dragging the hose to each tree and bush,
spraying the yard in high arches,
our walks to the corner store
for a snack and a soda.

Forty steps from the kitchen door
to the wilderness of our backyard.

    I learned to rest once the sun warmed
the part in my hair. Eat something. Enjoy the coolness
under trees. Return to work.

The sun followed me from beginning to end.

Then, my father
changed.

    His face pained each time he saw me.
And when I went out into the yard
he returned me,
sometimes even walking me there
himself, his hand circling my arm as
he led me back up the walkway.
Again and again,
to the house, to my mother.

Her space was the kitchen.
    Sideways sun from a small
window above the sink.
Always a little cold. Its pale light,
flung across floor tiles for maybe an hour.
Never meeting my eyes.

I was twelve when I started.
    Little was said
but I felt the moon rise within me,
like an electric current, the wind
falling short, just before the wall of me,
just before the storm in me.

date night

bourbon and some Isley brothers
then her arms drape across his shoulders
his hands resting at her hips

    dissolving
       the yells

    face slap

        hidden knives
           of yesterday

clumsy advances
nervous legs

hesitant cherubs,
    brother and I watch

corner house

Dark evenings and bad dreams stir again.
My father's mood falls back.

December marks his return from Vietnam.
    Sallow under eyes
a sign of his walks around the house's perimeter
in the middle of the night.

During the day he watches war documentaries
in the back room, his thumb presses
hard against the volume button
until the sound of helicopter blades thunders
against our bedroom walls.

This is how we celebrate Christmas.
I knot strings pulled from the hem of my dress   quiet
so as not to trip the wire
haphazardly coiled within him.

He's set a bomb under this house
    Mom says
and it's ticking away at us.[1]

---

[1] Twenty years later:
Do you know where Mom keeps her gun?
    Brother motions pillow and wall,
    the space between.
Do they have one or two?
    Raised shoulder, eyebrow lifts. *Why?*
She pulled a gun on Dad Friday night.
    I just found out from the neighbor.

anthropology

Zavala County soil is light in the north, loamy to the south.
Clay subsoil just beneath. Rich grasses fed by undercurrents
push from the Nueces and Rio Grande through limestone.

The Coahuiltecan lived on mussels and snails from nearby creeks.
Tonkawas ventured through, following buffalo, bear, and antelope.
Comanches chased Lipan and Mescalero Apache into this clearing.

Mustangs carved out the Wild Horse Desert, their lineage
a breeding between Northern Mexican wild herds and lost horses
of 17th century Spanish expeditions. So many, they owned the land.

General Antonio López de Santa Ana followed the Nueces
on his way to the Alamo. The land was forming a place
in this terrain between cultures—would try to choose a side

but never could. Grasslands gave way to livestock, abundant
once train tracks cut into the ground. Cows, horses,
and sheep so numerous, people living among them were ghosts.

Artesian wells brought in farming on lands cleared by hooves.
Speculators bought 96,101 acres. Created Crystal City,
named after its clear springs. An international call for settlers began.

Spinach grew in abundance. Cotton replaced native grasses.
Tangled groupings of pecan trees, lost to discovery: crude oil.
Those working the land grew in their support for Pancho Villa.

The town became two: Crystal City and Crístal.

Blame it on talc-faced Porfirio Díaz or the Mexican Revolution
or the new farms' call for workers—attracting Mexicans,
their homes built on borrowed land.

Split in two: one for whites, one for brown. Even when
the internment camps filled up during the war. When,
for a short time, the enemy wasn't a neighbor.

The separation burst into the Crystal City Revolts, poll taxes, loss.
If this earth were cut up for all, it would leave its bones uncovered
in the streets, its dust cloaking everything, lining the main drag.

* * *

From Interstate 83, back streets spur out
into grandmother's neighborhood. My father's mother.
Her desire tethered to the security of a house.

My father quit school, pooled money from odd jobs, enough
for a six-pack and sandwiches for a twelve-year-old's weekend.
Left alone most of the time, his face a duplicate

of the unknown man, his father—a reminder for the others.
The husband disappeared, made my father an outcast: locked
in a closet, or if he could run, left to sleep outside.

His curse boomed throughout the small town around him.
He managed what he could, made expected choices:
    wife   kids   job

but hurt them all. He knew no other way. Someone needed to pay.
The police told him to go—before an arrest could be made.
Didn't say goodbye to anyone before joining the army.

Crystal City gave more than its share to Vietnam. Gave so many
they ran out of parks and streets and dead ends to name after them.
The city more ghost than breath, more dogs howling at the Del Monte

horn than workers within its walls. There was no other work in this city.
When there was nothing else, there was spinach. Spinach
to grow the body strong. All this city needed were the bodies.

* * *

The playground across the street from his childhood house was a savior.
During visits we lunged our bodies out to the hardened ground
or walked its perimeter, like surveyors on the surface of Mars.

Not one inch of shade that whole block. Better in the unforgiveable sun
than to stay in his mother's dark house with its artifacts: a hardened fist
of ribbon candy sitting in the iridescent orange bubble dish,
the plastic-protected yellow gold velour couch. Grandpa Joe's recliner.

I burned the backs of my legs on the merry-go-round
while my brother threw sand down the slide to soften its heat.
The canvas swings in their own back and forth despite windless days.

We took turns pushing the other into the pale sky. Our fingers tight
around the chain, even through the jump: momentary weightlessness.
This is cowboy country, we said, as we waited for tumbleweeds
to skip along the flat compacted earth.

We considered our inheritance by what was visible:
translucent scorpions braving the hot sidewalks,
winged ants following one another without end.

Beneath this park, the story of ashes, of a burned house
on a block where all the houses burned in one way or another.
Me, in my yellow bikini, sitting in the red rider I filled with water.

My brother and me taking turns walking up and down the sidewalk,
the water hose following us, a constant pour over our feet.
And still the August sun swells skin. Red sand shifting into footprints.

house fire

Mom didn't tell Dad about the fire. Not right away.
Didn't call him at work to come home. Yet, when he arrived
he found all the doors open on a cold New Year's Day.

When he walked in, his joke about burnt dinner fell away
at the sight of smoked walls in the kitchen,
hallway, and into the bedrooms.

He wanted to know what happened, but Mom downplayed it.
It looks worse than it is. Not really a fire.
More smoke than anything.

Earlier in the day my brother played with his toys.
Mom and I were in the kitchen preparing a New Year's dinner.
Cleaning through black beans, I removed stones and broken bits,

glided them along the table with my palm into a heavy pot.
My brother ran out from the bedroom in a storm,
swiping past Mom's hip, *I'm going to go play outside!*

We fried up the pork roast, its crackle adding saltiness to the air.

      A low rumble of smoke

            seeping into the hallway   the living room,

black and grey   glided along the stream of cold air.

We didn't notice until it arrived in the kitchen,
bloomed up into the warm air.

Mom jolted up, ran to my bedroom.
Blackened walls, the low space heater on fire, my plastic dolls
melting on top, each with its own enflamed limbs, hair.

She turned off the gas, opened the doors and windows,
rushed back to push me outside. Smoke rolled out to the street.
I didn't get to see my dolls, but imagined arms and legs melting

down into the heater's grates, blond hair a soft, glistening nest.
My brother had played with them, laid them on the heater.
At the sound of our shouting, of his friends shouting,

my brother came running back. Smoke dissipated into
crackling meat and warming sofrito and water and black beans
and olive oil.

Dad arrived just as we calmed. He was ready to beat him
even before he knew who was responsible. Already, Mom was coaxing
with a long weekend and the coming dinner.

Still, he whispered: *He's trouble. I know it.*
In the days after, Mom soaped the walls,
chose paints and started to cover up.
Layers and layers over smoke.

bird calls

my brother has taken to hunting   he enjoys the quiet wait,
his back against a tree trunk, his eyes searching the leaves above
for movement

       a bird hops along a branch

my brother's hand cocks the bb gun
he pulls the barrel to his eye   and fires

he rarely misses but this particular blue jay is brisk
his wings a shock against the bristle of the pecan tree's canopy

I watch him
thankful he is occupied
thankful the bird has escaped

I call out to him
real hunters don't shoot and leave their dead
they kill to provide, to feed themselves

his face sours
and we have two days without shooting

in those two days he is a menace,
his feet near trampling me, his voice an echo of mine,
he pushes his body into my room
       and I scream at him
and at this circumstance:
this is summer vacation and we are ruthless animals

* * *

       the blue jay is the first to escape
after four deaths, a robin among them

each paraded through the house after
their song alerting him   and he showed me each one,
their feathers still soft save for the small charcoal
hole in the chest

     I'm surprised there's so little blood
just the dark red circle hollow and its darkness

Look what I got! I shot it!

each time his boasts followed by quiet
and I was thankful

* * *

I am resting at a cabin
overlooking the Blanco River   again shallow
after days of rain

the birds call out in the mornings
turkey vultures circle, the herons
with their clicks along the water's edge

at dusk there are families of deer too, cautiously nearing

I consider the possibility of bloodshed if my brother were here.
     It's hard to reconcile the hunter and destroyer within him
from the inconsolable boy desperate to be good at something

* * *

my father was an occasional hunter   I remember the deer,
back legs tied between two twin pecan trees   body hanging
the terrible arch of its hind legs, its throat fragile, loose
         the bloodletting and the bucket to collect it

* * *

        I remember the smell of every dead thing
we've come across   perfumed moldy fruit skin
    musky and just rained on dirt

* * *

my brother now thinks of himself as a provider
    lays out a frying pan, spatula, seasoning mix and oil
feathers on the greying bird plucked
her small chest open

        there's the sizzle

    it is days before I can look him in the face

only then does my mom remind him birds can have disease,
worms

I hope this one does

epicenter : 12

Two boys kissed me.
I felt   nothing   thought I should feel wonder, some question
    gain an understanding.
I barely remember their thin lips.

My cousin, attractive and with his handful of girlfriends, had promised
to kiss me, had managed to do more.
This much came out after,
as everyone in the family soon learned.

This is what happens when mother calls the cops.

My grandmother would say later that I must have asked for it,
been desperate enough to offer myself to him.
    What would a handsome man in his twenties want with her?
This is part of recorded history.

    What is not: that I wanted the idea of a kiss
   not from him but from   anyone
because I had already suffocated that part of myself.
I was twelve. I could not afford feeling.

He returned to the house several times within a window of months.
Always sitting close but at arm's length.

The last time he visited—before everyone knew what he was trying—
my father took us to the lake to meet him. We were trying to fish
but I gave up and threw the bait straight into the water.

He came back to the house with us,
meaning my brother and I sat in the truck bed holding
his motorcycle, while they sat up front drinking their beers.
At the first turn the bike skidded, fell onto me.
I screamed. They had thought me capable
of holding a man's weight.

That night he invited me to the spare bedroom.
I thought I had already carried so much
I could also hold this, this body's response.

What did I know about feeling wanted?

For so long I carried shame
in wanting to be seen.

sleep

We hope for night to finally arrive,
put us to bed, tidy up
the ruin of this day.

     Me with two pillows.
My brother, his footed pajamas.
My mother cradled in exhaustion and an electric blanket.

My father cannot sleep. He sits   at the kitchen table.
The streetlamp's light filtered in and cutting across his chin.
His breath sharp. His sullen hands,
   his fingers spread
along the wood top,
waiting.

fisheyes

the unblinking eye, framed
by natural dark pigment,
deep enough to make the white seem alien,
a skin like oiled rubber or curdled milk

and his iris something more than black
something endless and unforgiving

        my father
        but not my father

his fisheyes floating—
bulbous, seething
blood-filled
but heartless

effects

knives, wrapped in a dish towel, hidden under the sink[1]

unlocked door[2]

dinner at the table[3]

silence[4]

---

[1] He's coming home, hide the knives, once lined up in the utensil drawer, their points away from hands, each blade a silvery sheet.

[2] A locked door makes him even more angry. Unlock what you can or just open the doors. open windows. Let everything be open.

[3] He'll call from work, say he's on his way. This gives 12 minutes. have dinner ready. It can't be a minute late.

[4] There are kids, have them help with picking up the house then send them out or to their rooms. the television off. If the house is quiet he too may stay quiet.

the house next door is in flames | two

                just this last year

           houses all over
           have been going up in flames

              squatters

    houses are matchsticks, nearly touching
meant as temporary military housing
bundled together

                we are told to stand outside
                already there is blistering on the roof
                    and along the wall

                water spray turns vapor

in the far corner of the yard
the flames rising, rising

          as men walk through the house, their boot prints
          clustered at the doorways

                        there was nothing I could do
                          shaking, my body hot
                            against the cold air

epicenter : 9

under the cloudless frost of night,
between Christmas and the last frost,
between midnight and 2 a.m.,
the cold of the car's banquette front seat
through my pajamas finally wakes me

before: my mom's careful hand at my shoulder
her voice reached through my sleepiness
get up, mija   get up, come on
   we have to go

she roused my brother too, who
still with eyes closed, uncovered himself, sat up
and jumped down from the bunk bed
without questioning

the house, the wood floors so cold   we followed
through the kitchen, the patio, to the car,
   my mother's hands   slowly opened
each door   closed   with a hush

she pulled the keys from her pocket, wrapped them
in her fist   silent   the car turned over
headlights off

now   a shadow   in front of us   my father
had been asleep   a shovel
bangs against the windshield
once
   then again

he screams but there is only the windshield
    its tender webbing,
its legs and waves shine silver from the streetlamp's light,
lines stretch into the landscape forever   for a moment
I think: *Is he trying to hit me?*

                  then the light passes through
everything is light   the car's hollow brilliant
I can see now   we are in a cage   gilded, impossible cold
mist falling like lace   against a backdrop of deep blues
and the shadows of trees

my mother says only *come*
    delicate fingers return us to our beds
my mother's voice gone   gone
the gentle whispering

sunday afternoon

We are young and my brother has started watching WWE.
I trip. I always trip. By the time I'm 18 I've sprained one ankle
or the other 7 times.

I'm 13 and trip turning the corner from my bedroom to the dining room.
My brother lunges on top of me, pressing his entire body against my back

while he yells *What do you feel?* and I tell him
Nothing. And he asks again, his shoulders in it now too,

his legs straddling me, his hips pushing forward his hands
holding my arms down *Do you feel it?*

and still I say no.

    Furious, he jumps off,
    and bolts

and again I say *no*.

coupled

My fingers push against my father's bulging throat.
I pin him to the kitchen wall.

This is one lesson I had to learn in my mother's honor,
even while my mother tried to keep the house comfortable:
paying for the broken windshield with grocery money,
cooking meals even if no one ate,
hiding knives.

With our clothes in the backseat, we left town.

In the front seat, her talk as fast as her driving,
she says *Don't let a man define you.*
Don't allow yourself to be lost in a relationship.

I waited for relief
while my mother and her lover
slept late in the back bedroom.

The small rental house, one of three in a clearing,
offered her the chance that another man might have
what she needed. If only she could name it.

La Vernia, TX

I don't want my eyes open here. I don't want to dress for school
or to help my brother with breakfast. I'm not smart enough
for the school here. The teacher gives me work to finish later
because I can't finish it during the day.

When the school bus stops at the house the other kids remind me
this is where I live. One of three cement square houses circling
a cement water fountain collecting only infrequent rainwater.
I won't eat what my mom cooks but go to the neighbor's,
a native woman with braids and a sweet voice. Or I'll eat
at both houses until my belly painfully pulls itself
from my body.

I don't care if my classwork is done. I notice the sunset, its light
cuts through the front room's one window, shifts from yellow
to orange to purple. I sleep in the lower bunk of the doorless room.
I pretend not to hear my mother's voice. I don't say good night.

pilgrimage

My mother stands at the water's last wave to the shore.
Her heels sink in. Water softens resistance.

She asks for forgetfulness, maybe, of all that has happened;
she is asking for salt water to help clear her path.

    So much happens where I am a bystander.
So many fleeting looks I'm unable to decipher.

My mother lost her mother, Cora, when she was young.
Something in the crippled arms of mesquite trees that surprises her,
how they soothe despite their broken bodies. Tendrils of roots beneath,
strong taproot. Impossible to uproot.
Cutting only hardens their clutch.

We drove back home just as winter clouds began to set.
It's evening in the shadows of mesquite trees.

Shadows that follow us home, despite the promise an ocean offers.
The breeze mimics ocean waves across the grasses.

        Sometimes I imagine brilliant red syruped hearts
released from the sky, a jelly creature sinking into branches,
punctured by mesquite fingers.

Back home, mesquites continue their dance: how two
come together, how another offers its canopy to the street.

Wrapped in speckled shade, they root themselves
beneath the house foundation, pull at deep wells of salt water.

hibiscus

Mama rented a duplex in southern Florida with high, narrow windows
only on the south wall. I couldn't see anything through them save a pale
blue sky, skittered clouds, and red-orange hibiscus flowers. She packed
us up to move away from the husband and was helped by a man who
once worked the radio for incoming single-engine airplanes heavy
with cocaine, their bellies bumping across the low sky.

We didn't have much even if the boyfriend gave some. All he bought
with funneled money was in someone else's name. Good thing that
plant gave a new flower each day. Then rested each evening.
Lanky pine trees in the distance sway in the bleaching heat.

My brother grew into a bull shark. I helped with a new job while
learning the fundamentals in art class. The quick schedule I made
    bus   school   bus   home   work   home
to occupy my time wasn't enough. On days I didn't work I would
put on my bathing suit and sit in the yard with a radio, hoping for a tan.
Since I was from Texas, neighbors asked what I'd done with my horse.

It was commonplace for alligators to run loose in the neighborhood.
The grass clutched sand desperately. I spent my time color coordinating
girls' wallets at the department store and ate pudding during work breaks.

Those hibiscus petals weighed down.
Unwilling to open by the time August hit.

On Saturday nights, the boyfriend comes over and we go for a drive
along the Tamiami Trail to West Flagler. My brother and me in the back,
watching the clouds through the moon roof. My mother so far away.
The boyfriend talks about moving to Puerto Rico but eventually,
we return to my father. Phone hangups trail us for a few months,
the boyfriend hoping for my mother's voice.

what my father buries

What my father buries—what circles the bones of this house, reaching its furthest points:

Two coke bottles from the opening of Fiesta Texas, marked with the glory of a new rollercoaster and painted fireworks. A snow globe with its white flecks glittering the city skyline at the shake of a wrist. A city that's seen snow three times since 1971. A plastic sandwich bag archiving three semi-intact curls of red brown hair from my three-year-old head. (Maybe my first haircut. Maybe sacred and rooting me to this house.)

Two milk bottles filled with marbles so tight they make no sound when handed off. A bb gun, its pump handle half-cocked and rusted. My mother's *House Beautiful* magazines. My brother's rodeo boots from third grade. A cigar box with centavos, centesimos, pence, pesos, and francs. Lots and lots of beer cans thrown into corners. Corner house. Mesquite tree lounging in the front yard shows its roots as a maze beneath this house.

Last week a man walked along the underside of this house, removed flooring, and straightened floorboard before tile could be set flush with the hallway. My father sat nearby, supervised his work, and through the floor, offered a history of its two-inch duplex nails. Last week another man in a white truck followed a neighbor woman in her silver car from the highway to the access road to this cross street. No stop signs. He pulled ahead of her and shot at her twice. The heat flashed through her arm and folded into her stomach. She managed to drive a block away for help. Police in search. Hispanic male. 5'8". Heavyset.

my mother is the center of this house

Having worked for this yard, planted its trees, set the wooden fencing,
fortified this house, the plumbing and electrical wiring through it,
kept the peace, fed the kids, worked a job, sometimes two,
soothed the husband,

    my mother somehow kept the walls upright.

She falls back into the sofa for a moment.
The pier and beam foundation of this house yields to the parched ground.
Cracks climb along the corners. Gaps still show, despite all her work.

In early morning light, dust circles her, highlighting the subtle air.
Every corner of this house shackles her.

When she pulls her arms in to warm herself, the walls bellow in.
This braced life, this hold never sleeps.
These hands never rest.

bitter oranges

This is what has made her mad, she realizes. That she took the role
she never really wanted, that it weighed so much more
than the lilt of freedom.

Losing freedom is worse than never having it.
Maybe.

I shouldn't have had kids, she says,
not looking in my direction.

* * *

Her hair. She says she has horse's hair and we laugh
because horses always look supersoft.

More like skunk or goat. Thick.
Bristly but shiny.

It moves as one, like an animal breathing
—in then out—as fingers pass through.

* * *

Usually soap, and skin dewy, fresh from the shower.
The scent lingered on her skin for hours.

Or sweating onions—on her hands.
Or the cold, wet smell of meat.

And sometimes a distant cigarette. Hers, yes,
but also like an unfortunate walk through smoke.

She always smoked outside, stepping away from the path
of her exhales. A dance of avoidance.
In thrall to the trajectory of wind,
the power of her own lungs.

* * *

We—my brother and I—are side conversations
to whatever my parents had promised themselves.

There was nothing to carry that did not arrive taped up,
stapled, bruised, or tied together. Even us.

I just suffered through.

She says to me: *You are so nice. I give advice and you listen
but you don't take any of it. You'll do what you want, I guess.*

* * *

black beans
Chanel No. 5

swallowed consonants
painted walls

keds and smooth calves
broken windshields

* * *

Minnesota an outlier. Cuba made myth.
Homestead sometimes, Miami when she feels free.
Florida, in one way or another, always.

Central Texas an endurance, like bitter oranges.

Dulce de naranja agria.

Skins peeled away, hands sticky with their oil.
Each segment membrane spooned out.
Rinds cut into quarter moons.

Boiled, over and over in fresh water,
they become ghosts of themselves.

Doused in sugar and boiled down once more.
A sweet made from impossible tartness.

* * *

I don't speak much when I am young.
My mother's friends tell her I'm quiet,
that I'm a good girl.

It's the middle of the night. A school night.
My father is yelling. My brother has run away.
Again.

My mother takes me with her as we drive around looking.
Why can't he be like you? she would say.
You never give me any trouble.

the house next door is in flames | three

    arson
            they say

not a firework
or electrical

      who called the fire department? the arsonists themselves?
          a kind of Christmas gift
      the two minutes gifted
when we could have fallen into deeper sleep,
smoke blanketing our bodies

there are trucks in the street
water all over

and we are allowed back into the house where we
set up a false normalcy   at the kitchen table
coffee and the offer of a sandwich   cheese maybe
cheese will ground my stomach   the kitchen smells
like smoke   the only room with lights on, plumes
moving through the walls
though the fire is not done swallowing us
      wood snapping   voices back and forth
outside   water searing

and in that noise my mother's voice echoes,
are you okay?

her mouth is a hollow   a resignation
rolling

epicenter : 14

    I wake up   split open
and raw.
        Lightning
For a moment
      brings me back.

My mother calls out   ,   late for school. I push
                heavy limbs   . My head won't stop

    night before   trouble[d] sleep   .

                In my parents' bedroom   low,
the light   in and out   At least one

I walk across   the door is
locked.   pills.
orange, round tabs,   blue and red gelatin capsules,
small white ones.   hot, clammy.

                                        one by one. No water.

            trouble
will end.

The shock of waking in the morning   .   school.

* * *

       doubts   soft
girl: uncommunicative, yellow-skinned, poor, not especially pretty.

                                  I knew no other way   .
                         /   /

this never happened.
and then I had no choice.

Suddenly
               pulled   memory   shut

        didn't want   .   didn't want to say anything.

His mother said I had asked for it,
  That he could

* * *

I couldn't
  I didn't

          I reached for my head
          wasn't communicating.

     to the nurse.

         pills—a lot of them—after.

My mother came to school to pick me up.

* * *

     I just wanted   the quiet.

echoes

My mother had a visitor today. Someone she remembered
as a young woman. The daughter of the previous owner of our house.
    Sand colored hair, round cheeks, pained smile.
She grew up in this house.

    She was four when they moved in. 1944.
Her room became my room. I was four when we arrived too.

They sat together on the side porch, in April's early heat.
She mostly spoke. My mother mostly listened.

Her father drank. He lost job after job.
Her mother was a teacher working year round
to keep the house together, to keep food on the table.

She takes a breath to enjoy the porch, the plants. painted fence.
Those were impossible things when she was growing up.
There was no extra money for decorations.

Some nights they were lucky they could protect their mother,
his arms pushing between them. Punches find their way to her.

    It's funny—what we convince ourselves is a marker of growth—
that having made it out is victory enough. The life hard won.

My mother tells me this as though it's the plot of a soap opera.
My face unfurls. We do not say those walls were primed
and ready for us. Our new family.

We refuse the conversation we owe ourselves,
the belief in like attracts like.

This woman, after so many years and her parents gone, sits outside,
her laughing—almost animal, almost joyous in comeuppance,
even distanced by time—surprises me, sends a cackle
of fingers down my back. Almost seventy now, she eyes me
and claims the center bedroom on her way out.

poker face

lined along the refrigerator door
four, sometimes more, lipsticks
in various shades of red
    carmine
    ruby
    spice
    rouge
        because they last longer
            my father's mother says

enticing totems awaiting their call

as a young woman, full-lipped mouth painted in berried red,
she had her haze of evenings out and potential husbands
when hers was away at war

she makes use of a life that would have otherwise left her unsatisfied

now, as an old woman, her thin lips hold a noxious spittle
the deep clicks of her tongue push against
tight-pursed lips

deep red
    jutting at my father
        who could never measure up
    or at my step-grandfather
        who gave her all he could

she always squinted her eyes just before
she revealed what she felt was true
    black honey almost
her language from a war long fought
those cold lipsticks outlasting their purpose

bearing gifts

My father gets homesick and wants to drive to Crystal City.
This means my mother drives since he needs to drink

for the two-hour journey. We might never stop for snacks
or restrooms. Going home is bad enough. To stop means

this trip will take even longer. Mom insists and we take a break
near a fruit vendor. Tan truck backed up on the roadside,

offering grapefruits and oranges in 4-foot plastic netting.
He's paying and suggests his mom will want some.

The bags settle, in a thud, on the floor of the back seat.
Our feet don't quite reach them.

My mother soon notices their smell. One is rotten.
The vinegar moving through our closed car.

Puckered flesh falls into itself.
We continue driving:

growing mold scent, flat, treeless horizon,
water illusions along the folds of pale grey roads.

We want to tear through the bags, throw each globe
out the window, leaving juice splatters along the roadside

to mark our way back home. We want
to pluck out the offending fruit,

hold it as a trophy and scream out.
But we stay seated.

This is my father's offering to the home he hopes to find
in his mother's face. Her eyes avoid him.

Oranges carry a secret in their skins.
When peeled back to reveal the flesh,
they spit.

Neighborhood gossip, pan dulce and a call to his brother,
who comes by from the next town over. He is a buffer

sitting across the enamel kitchen table,
a plate of oranges there between them.

grandmother mouth

1.
I have my mother's mother's teeth—square, off-colored things.

Cora, the caretaker of her neighborhood and her family, foretold death
through her dreaming mouth.
Each falling tooth a loved one sleeping in those heavy rooms in Cuba,
their walls painted a leaded blue;

Cora says there are fated spaces. Predetermination loosens,
leaves a place that grows into emptiness.

2.
Anita, my father's mother, is a reminder that clichés have their truth:
only the good die young.

Blaming the youngest for why she was left single,
her pursed lips present in every photo from the 1950s on.
She lays in her bed at the old folks home
—no phone, no roommate can stand her—
she talks about those who aren't visiting her.

Anita says we don't look like the rest of the family, wonders aloud
if my mother has black relatives because of our rounded bodies,
because of our full mouths.

She holds her lips tight, doesn't want to lose the poison
salivating from her mouth. She's not done yet.

starless

The sixteen-year-old who would become my mother had, within two years, left Cuba as part of the mass exodus to Miami, where her mother died of an aneurysm, where she then moved with my grandfather to St. Paul where, at 18, she returned to night school to finish her GED. She bumped into then married my father, only 23 and just returned from Vietnam with a GI Bill that paid for his certificate in auto body repair.

Her dating prospects in Southern Florida before the move were:

The Argentine doctor who would be gone for weeks to visit his mother,

The neighborhood butcher and his offers of extra chops and oxtail,

The furniture salesman whose family owned what would become a chain of high-end furniture stores in South Florida called El Dorado, and

The printmaker turned narcotraficante who flew in drugs from South America through the Florida swamplands.

To this day my mother will say: *If only I had known more English then. I wouldn't have ended up with that man.*

* * *

The snow. Endless. Releases
memory as it obscures the wild

landscape. This place—impossible
to believe it is tethered

to faraway rows of palms through this girl.
This snow. Milky. Wistful.

Cold is a dangerous thing.
It will swallow any remaining fight

found in the willful girl.

* * *

She only sees what she wants.
The body tired from anticipating.
Moon-shadowed life.
   Starless drifting.

She understands the heated rush.
Appreciates the admiration, the touch
—*Baby*—toward a kind of love.

   She didn't know what kind of man she wanted
until she knew this was not the kind she wanted.

Something slow is ideal because this life has burned through
so much of her already. *Believe me*, she says, matter-of-factly,
when it comes to love it's easier to go with what can be known.

That or find a way
to wipe yourself clean
of all of it.

record player

on rainy days Tom T. Hall sings about what he loves:
little baby ducks, bourbon in a glass, and grass

the crisp shuffle of the needle almost skips *and I love you*
but dad is there to sing it right

    and we all laugh

on bruised mornings my mother wants the loneliness
of The Eagles or, on particularly terrible afternoons
The Pointer Sisters, who sing about a slow hand
and my mom dances in the kitchen, bumping
against us and against my dad's anger
until he is stone, until he walks out,
my mother laughing and laughing

safe house

My brother isn't allowed to know where I live
and my mother's instructions for dealing with him
are cautionary tales.

If you see him at a store and he follows you out
don't go home right away. Don't ever give him money.
Don't tell him when you'll be meeting up with other family.
If you give him a ride somewhere do so only if it takes him away
from your house. Better yet, don't let him in your car at all.

And if any story from his mouth starts with *see what happened is*
cut it off there, offer some drive-through combo meal,
and say goodbye.

If you want to reach him, you'll have to try another day
because this one will likely end in a combination of
any of the following:

beat up girlfriend,
borrowed car set on fire,
someone's car radio stolen from a Walmart parking lot,
cleaning supplies for making meth, bought at that same Walmart,
another baby announcement during Christmas,
a drive-by or the story of one,
or something left in your backyard for safe keeping.

And if he starts with *tell me the truth*
he already knows the answer
and wants to catch a liar in their lie.

Friends with my brother means you are now worse off
than if your car seats had just burned away.

ode to the broken clavicle

my brother holds a scattering of broken clavicles in his palm
his lips whisper across each tender reed

    resting in a light sleep, warm cavities of bone
secret keepers of the possible:

  arms outstretched,
the lightness of this flight
gone

    instead cradled secrets
and fists crashing
down

    startled, each girl shudders
unable to escape

his words splintering
into their hollow

until they burst open
brittle,
gasping

      there is no story left in a broken clavicle
      no divination for its caged girl

my father calls to me

For an eternity my father barely spoke. Whether provocation or humor,
he would not let a thing into him but this new behavior shows
at the middle of his life. The ways we have learned to lie to ourselves.

As a child, he was thrown into the closet by his brother and sister.
Scared of the dark, years later, his flashbacks held in fists.
The desperation to get his point across.

He is a physical magician, pulling matter from the air
until it's knives or dishes or handfuls of hair—whatever can be

jettisoned.   Other times, no shortage of words,
his voice a study in ballistics, his beliefs condensed to *me / not me*.

    I walk into his room at the long-term hospice center.
I don't know if he's awake. Medical equipment keeps its rhythm

and there is a whisper from the television at the far back.
Please god, don't let me get this way, I think.

There is no medicine for his seizure. It sits at his chest,
exaggerating his heartbeat. I place my hand there.

His breath quick at my fingers' reach. *Dad, do you remember me?*
Yes, he mutters, *Jo Anne*.   In his house there was never a normal.

His head bob is a call. *Water -*, he says.
    Wa t -e-r.   He asks for it but there isn't any.
This whole room is meant to leave him without help.

He used to make fun of my Spanish, how I dropped the end syllables,
like my mother. *Pinche Cubana*, he would say, and laugh at his insult.

When he is lucid he's reminded he must clean up his own mess.
He'd rather not be reminded.

Now he churns mouthfuls of words as I sit nearby.
He is speaking to me, I think, then realize he is facing the corner.

Occasionally his eyes lower to mine. Despite this distance, his cadence
is recognizable even if I understand little of what he does say.

He never listened to me. Here I am, listening, but unable to latch on
until he says my name

and it's a rubber ball echoing hard against the walls
and we are both momentarily woken up from the sleepiness
that fills the room like a gas.   His dinner is on a rolling tray
five feet away. He can't have pushed it away.
His fingers tighten as though cradling a cup.

I slip my fingers into his palm to jolt him again and offer dinner.
His voice is momentarily easy.   I assume this means yes.

Everything a softness, whether meat or juice or pudding. When offered,
it sits on his lips or rolls from the side of his tilted mouth.

I thought his state would bring desperation   the food, the mumbling,
the incessant, low beeps from the machines   but he hasn't looked past

this foothold   this   this is how he will be at the end of his life
—alternating between apologies and anger—after having stayed quiet

when things mattered.   I understand now
the need to make a sound in this place.   Any sound.

Before it's too late.

bruising

        Assault with a deadly weapon—
    my brother's two hands

at her neck.
One year ago.

And we have just learned
it could mean 20 to 25 years.

How long does the bruising along her jaw leave its tracing?
    Two weeks? Three?

What conversation he must have managed
as his fingers first spun themselves
around her neck.

    I am driving as I consider this. Driving without breath.
Purple blue flames of feathers suddenly cross the street, carried by the wind.
A bruising of feathers.

I'll never know where they came from
or why they are here, now,
crossing me.

    The deep shake of breath returns in lumps.

How long did she have to deny his handiwork until the cops believed her?
How long until she believed it never happened?

And what did she receive in exchange but the weight of him— all
shoulders, arms, palms, knees—and the lightness of stolen breath, faint
    a blossom in her brain.
I am home.
I managed it, despite tears.

Vines climb the fence of my house: pink heart cages—antigonon—
and open blossomed blue trumpets—laurel clock vine.
This is spring into summer. After so much rain.

     Damage must be dealt with
before growth is possible. The clinging vines
browned by winter must be pulled away.

This is my world, again now, so close to wreckage.

here is what I've learned

Choose. Sometimes a minute at a time.

Once chosen give everything to it.[1]

Consider what's necessary.[2]

Reconsider how we arrive at this moment.[3]

My body   this island   so small.
I don't know how to pay it all
back.[4]

---

[1] No matter that I may wake up with a different choice.

[2] What do I need now? To lay down? To hear another's voice? To eat or drink something? To feel the wind on my skin?

[3] Life is a willful act. It is standing still. It is a step back and a breath. Or held breath across an ocean. An unloosening. Thinning roots. Piecemeal. Bruise. Cajole. Punishment. The promise of not falling apart.

[4] It is years before I realize there is nothing to pay back. And what we hold wasn't ours to hold at all.

friendly fire

the wood fence my father built up himself,
that my mother painted brick red each year

    f e n c e   l i n e

                  s i d e w a l k

    broken tailpipe   no gas   expired sticker
my brother's car   parked and unmoving days now

my father   standing outside   day or night
staring at the car   scanning the landscape,
his eyes move across   my brother's face   he sits there
     a kind of meditation

yelling at him when he comes in to use the water hose
or takes a tool from the shed

f e n c e   a kind of boundary   we don't come in,
my brother or me   my father's face is enough   to stop
but so is the physical line his mind has set

     I wait
for my mother to come out

we have planned for lunch together

    We greet each other with a one-armed hug
arms still in their forward movement
when

                get out of here
                    I've told you already

                                okay   *okay*

how many times do I need
to tell you?

just one more time

and his laughter   under his breath
and my mother and me watching
and Sergeant, the dog,
my brother at the far gate's entrance, still laughing   my father
walking toward him   my brother, turning to leave   my father,
his steps moving to a run   and both still with their mouths open

      and my mother moves from me   toward them
      and I am left at the gate   along the fence alone

gun

he has a gun   my brother
has a gun

      and everyone stops

my brother's arm steadies the gun
though the weight of it (or of all of this) leaves him shaking
his wrist falling   his lips moving
but I can't read them   I can't hear him

    my father screaming

then he falls back

I see my father   and I step toward him
the bullet straight
from the gun through the dog's foot
and lodged into my father's calf
                my mother is screaming now

I can't hear her but her mouth is moving and I know she is saying

he shot him he shot him
oh my god he shot him

my brother looks back
jumps the fence

why? why?

the dog whimpers

my mother holds my father's shoulders   *why?*

my father on the ground
clutching his leg

I grab her face
look in her eyes
she is staring into nothing

I tell her
call 911
go get the phone
call 911
GO

she nods
but does not move

Look at me!   Look at me!
Go inside and call the police.

unsteady, she runs into the house

I look over but my brother is gone   he's run down the street
my father groans
and my mother hands me the phone   an operator's voice on the line
>   *Is anyone there?*
>   *Is this an emergency?*

I cup it to my ear. I can hear the office noises behind her.
The steady white noise.   *My name is Jo Anne.*
                    I live at 1632 El Monte.
                    My brother, Raul,
                    just shot my father in the leg.

                    Send an ambulance.

There are questions coming through the line but I cannot answer.
She says my name.
Once. Then again.

I drop the phone.
I'm starting to lose it.

The operator says my name again.

This is why I don't answer to my name.

the house next door is in flames | four

        something sweet, I say
     to bring the spirit back to the body

         and some water
       to smother the fire within

to tamp down this early morning
and the forty years prior
in the house

    the soul of this house
    framed in dry wood
    its aches opened
    with every creak

and the plumes of smoke
rolling rolling
and rolling

lighting the sky
into false sunrise

plumes of smoke
rolling, rolling
up, into the night sky

flint

My brother arrives at my work,
leaving me to translate his rough hands and angular jaw
for the hesitant watching behind cubicle walls.

Gone are his youthful round eyes and sleepy pout.
His skin now ashy, weathered. His chin losing its edge.
Reddened skin tied tight. Straw-stuffed body waiting for a light.

Age has loosened his secrets.
Fear has built its nest within him.

He borders on homelessness.   Just in case,
dark clothes to hide and protect his body:
two pair of shorts, two pair of socks,
a button down, and t-shirt worn in layers
on a hot August day.

He's just released from jail and needs to make a call.
No message really, just a thanks to Mike or John or whoever
bailed him out this time.
This part isn't new. He's always thankful.

I offer coffee. Give my lunch to his blind hand.

The shape of our childhood has worn on him.
He bears the brunt of our anger and can't reconcile it within,
even as our stories are unraveling. We break repeatedly,
consider ourselves lucky to have managed a life.

His metallic eyes roam the landscape within
that softness is quivering   he cries without breath.

I have denied myself this hurt.
Like a firefly, I am pinned to his dark shirt.

amendment

My mother is mad at me.

By tomorrow, we will meet for lunch,
and things will be fine
until I say

I wasn't her savior when,
as a girl, I pushed
my father against the wall,
   my fingers
around his throat,

her curses, her laughter at this sudden twist.

   Rather, I was holding my own story back,
did not want the ending laid before me.

tinderbox

    It's a puzzle to craft: a candle maybe, or a cigarette,
and an accelerant—gas or alcohol. How do you
slow a fire down? Once it's had its first laps of air,
how do you hold its neck against its hungry gulps?
Fire takes the path it chooses, no matter what
the hands who have crafted the flame may plan.

    And how do we fit this open? You and me.
How often were we made enemies in our story? You, dark, tall
and menacing in a house that accepted anger as currency. Me,
short, pale, and quiet in a house that demanded it.

And when you snuck out of the house I was there, one
window down, listening to the quiet scratching of tennies
down the side of the house. And when you broke young
women apart, I could hear your voice through the wall,
talking with friends about the next one. And when you
were punished, locked in your room, I knew before
they did, about the stash hidden under your pillow.

We were children then. Or tried to be. I hoped the world
you followed could be put to rest, made something new.
But we aren't children now, are we?

To find out it was about a woman, a woman who wanted
to sell the house out from the owners—a woman who made
you mad because she'd gotten the better of you
and so the house had to be gone so that she
would go without. Your gift of punishment.

Still, when I think of all the ways a burning house
can make an appearance in someone's story,
I never thought I would be the one nearly gone
and you the one who laid the kindling.

slicing fruit

Cutting mangos into bite-sized pieces
in the kitchen that's yet to be painted.

The phone rings. Answering is an impossibility but,
despite sticky fingers, my mother's voice
chimes through.

The latest in a marriage deteriorating.
The story retold—a litany with its set responses.

How many difficult and different ways to say
The love isn't there. Was never there.

Never easily heard.

Pineapple next on the cutting board.
It's difficult to stop the years of giving in

and I need to stand outside for this, need the humidity of summer,
the shallow breaths of our upbringing—my mother's and my own—

This house, new to us, is full of dust. We keep sanding down
to its origin wood. Pine so thick it breaks the saw.

I need this kind of assurance.

Piquant scents waft through this house, juice coats my fingers.
My inheritance: the heaviness of lungs holding their inhalations.

collateral damage

                to not have been chosen

to have birthed a girl child
who could be loved
who was good and lucky too
was unexpected

        this family isn't known for good   or luck

   so I was pushed aside
    after she came through
here was a chance to start again
    for my mother   who could not mother
here a chance to love without worry about a man
hurting either of them

but people don't change   I was a reminder
of all she did not want to relive and so she shut me out

        until much later,
when my child walked through the house
a young adult with her own handicaps

      and my mother finally looks at me
and asks *why is she always angry?*
If her life was protected, why is she hard all the time?
as if to say *what did you do to mess this up for me?*

      And I refuse to answer.
If my voice wasn't valuable then why offer it now?
If she will not hear the answer she already knows—that anger,
like anything else, is inherited—why bother asking me?   Me,
who had to learn how to mother myself, and sometimes her,
and that child too?

staring contest

Mom wants to know why her eyes didn't win out.
My father's eyes an easygoing caramel.
My brother's whisky brown. Mine honey with green flecks.

She has green, intensely green, eyes with rings of hammered brass.
And if she fought you her eyes grew brighter still.
There was no war she could not win.

I start to explain the many possibilities for genetics
but her stare is capable of unlocking excuses.
Her squint never softens.

Anger is a serpent coiled within her, riling.

The world did not go her way.
She is a cold emerald in an underwater cave.
She is her own Bermuda Triangle.

my brother the pragmatist

My brother folds his shirts neat, stacks them in the back seat.
Every button of every shirt lined up, one atop the other.

His shoes are practical, take him from roofing work to nighttime
gatherings around the fire pit with friends.

My brother asks my mom to hold his money.
She doesn't offer interest, and holding comes with a lecture,
but he trusts her more than banks.

My brother rents apartments in our parent's names,
knowing they will take care of the yellowed kitchen walls
and small fire damage in the bathtub.

My brother works on his car most afternoons
and decides to remove the gas tank
since he won't have gas money this week.
He may as well keep up his skills.

My brother is looking for a new car.
He likes to drive with the windows down.
His revoked license and stolen plates an incentive
to take advantage of the day.

My brother welcomes another child. He refuses condoms.
He doesn't want to remove his girlfriend's right to choose.

My brother is in love with his girlfriend. If they break up
for a day or two he finds another girl because they are momentarily
out of love. *It is what it is*, he says.

My brother is the pretty one.
He always was.

blasphemy

When I don't deny, there are plenty of things to occupy me:

wishes for stars not visible in our city sky, endless chalk drawings
on sidewalks, kids flying all around.

My chin finds itself pressed against someone's breastbone,
their arms relaxing across my shoulders.

The suffocation of family gatherings on the side porch,
framed by the barbecue pit, radio speakers blaring,
sandals at the door's entrance.

The way my memory falters with each story, retold.
The truth of our selves braided between tangled shoulders.

I don't believe it when I'm told family knows best.

What they know is outward, a study in the way I behaved while young,
under close supervision. A source for altered memories
always recounted at the worst moments.

familiar

And all around you a vast terrain.
—GLORIA ANZALDÚA, FROM "LETTING GO"

We are each called in our own way.

My child, mind like a countryside, was born on a misty summer evening.
Sun long gone by the time she was truly in my arms.

Small thumps along the windowpane. Flickers in the humid night.
Lightning bugs mark a welcome path for her,

glimmer to illuminate her eyes, even in the darkest times.
My child protected.

* * *

We have been out.
    It's mid-August
and there is no getting away from
this heat.

The air is damp against our skin
but our throats are dry.

We need water
when the cool inside air
rushes us. We are breathless.

The air conditioner shakes this old house,
visits each room with its concentric calls.
Moves through our bodies too,
echoes in the water resting in our glasses.

There are moments when
we forget we are part of each other,
when we forget we are part of the larger world too.

We forget even the trees talk to each other,
protect each other. Without a word.

* * *

As a child, I would sit on just-rained walkway.
Knees up, arms hugging my shins.

Sometimes I waited full minutes for a trail of ants
to link back and forth, sharing gossip,
or watch a baby frog jump across.

Perhaps I thought of myself as their caretaker.
Perhaps just a witness who could say
yes, they did pass here
on a cool afternoon
just after a light rain

* * *

I remember telling her
our bodies are riddled with stars,
that the viscous within her is a concoction
—cool and dark—of life's insistence,
and so she doesn't need to struggle for so much
because the journey here
has been made
for her.

All she has to do is breathe in
and the galaxies circle again.

* * *

Small, winged creatures find me.
They sit on my morning papers,
walk across the dusty windshield
for attention.

Nameless beauties come to rest on my shoulder or palm.
Same with this child I had the joy to have raised.

How each has their movement on this land
that becomes the curve and sway of
their singular language.

How I have allowed their voices to move me.

How each vibration has changed me.

* * *

Porch light out. The sun gone now, an hour or more.
Cicadas congregate beneath streetlights.

Curious, how, in hearing them, I realize
how much I have missed their metallic howls

across the lawn, its echoing waves
roll from one side to the other.

And there's a rumble too, of a train, its belly lumbering—
still at a distance but closing in.

The tick tick tick of wheels turning.
At the edges of the lawn, a congregation of frogs.

Their greenblack skins a mirror to the stars unfolding
in this new night.

  Have they learned to sing?
Or, do they still need to find their reason for song?

      Such perfection
      in what is young.

Take, for instance, my daughter at the back of the house.
Her skin like unfolding flowers, her voice barely a whisper
but she reels through me like that train.

When she hurts
the center of me aches
though it's been years since she lived in my body.
Long enough that my body is new again
three times over.

The whole house is in darkness.
  Together, here, we become a study in geometry:
the frogs angle toward their home of grass and loamy soil,
just beneath the mailbox. The train long gone now, shifting
at the horizon. The chorus of cicadas weakening.
The rolling laughter from the back room.
My daughter, talking on the phone with friends.

She too, a small, glossy being, otherworldly
in the diffused light of evening
into night.

anticipation

I try to imagine a time in the future   when my child's children
will have something of mine they pass down, or a gift from my child,
something we once held, some charm or handkerchief
        a book, perhaps, a piece of jewelry

        can fingerprints stay ever present, despite layers and layers
of dust, of rumbled packaging paper
            I hope so   I hope they lay still along the surface
of whatever I may have ever held   like an errant hair, hardly missed
clinging smooth against smooth

        but this runs counter to our family's tendency
    to move, to leave anything with weight as a gift
for whoever has the current need

this is one way we claim our family:
to see who holds an affinity for books, who needs the cooking pot,
whose child can wear the clothes

but I can conjure something small to offer the future,
like the yellowed notebook paper carrying lyrics for a décima
in my grandfather's handwriting   held by his hands then mine
in hope there will be more writers in this family, that they will have
found a way to flourish through a string of letters

        but if there is nothing to pass on   let the charm
that pours through these bodies find their way   let the one ear
that bends awkwardly out make our stories accessible down the line
let the inherited feet we struggle against allow us to slow down,
trusting I walk with them

let them hold close what cannot be evaluated with a magnifying glass
or pinned to legacy   let them leave their own fingerprints
on the next life   and learn what is truly worth holding

unmasking

Here now, I think I understand Fall is a conjured thing, an impossibility
against the constant sun in the South Texas valley.   Yet, somehow,
cooler weather manages
              and my skin is aching for more.

Windows down, I attempt errands but each stop
becomes a kind of discovery—new places, a grove
of unexpected citrus trees—and music begs
to be sung.

          At stoplights
I contemplate the driver in the car next to me, who turns his head
then smiles. His wave and subtle nod beckon—so sad
he's in the turn lane
and I'm moving forward
                following the horizon.
     To one side the sun falling away,
to the other the surrounding darkness
of a blue whale, its entire body in dappled blues
churning into nighttime sky, then starlight, its hot heart
racing with me along Highway 83.

Possibilities are sticky things here.
They ease their way in,
past my walls.

     I have my walls.

I drive through the car wash, always skittish as I try
to get the front wheel into position. There seems only one way
but that can't be the truth. I'm sure I'll never make it
but still, somehow, each time, the wheel finds its way.

I don't believe our lives are so scripted.
If I did, I wouldn't be here now, having run my car
under blue and purple suds, picking up books from a friend,
and returning to a small apartment—my home for now—
while, in the approaching darkness,
the outline of birds circle a cluster of trees
in their delirious murmurations.

Alone in this place, alone but woven
into the insistence of the people here, constant
as bird caws, as stars bursting, constant
as our drowsy and constant sun,
and the wind reaching for my face,
building something within
I can't yet name.

                That blue whale following still,
its lumbering body crashing into the horizon.
Its heart matching mine, beat for beat.

Acknowledgements

These poems appeared in journals or magazines, sometimes in earlier versions or just portions of.

"bitter orange" *Writing the Mother Wound: A Mother's Day Anthology*
"Familiar" *Chachalaca Review*
"flint" and "my brother the pragmatist" *Huizache Magazine*
"half sun" *Imaniman: Poets Writing in the Anzalduan Borderlands*

With thanks to Anita, who understands and deserves/demands joy. Thanks also to early readers and friends ire'ne lara silva, Maribel Sanchez, and Valeka Cruz.

I am honored to have worked with Niki Herd, Virgil Suárez, and Emmy Pérez, each of whom helped deepen my skill but, more than that, through their example taught me to trust my writing voice.

Laura Van Prooyen, you have seen so much of this manuscript's trajectory. Thank you for your poetic doula skills.

About the Author

jo reyes-boitel is a poet and playwright, queer mixed Latinx, amateur hand percussionist, and parent. Nearly completing their MFA in Creative Writing at the University of Texas-Rio Grande Valley, they serve as a presidential fellow and teach undergraduate creative writing. jo is a fellow of Macondo and Voices of Our Nations (VONA). Their hybrid opera, "she wears bells", was chosen as a 2022 Guerilla Opera Virtual Festival finalist. Previous publications include *Michael + Josephine*, a novel in verse (FlowerSong Press, 2019), and the chapbook, *mouth* (Neon Hemlock, 2021).

For more information about jo and their work visit joreyesboitel.com.

www.ingramcontent.com/pod-product-compliance
Lightning Source LLC
Chambersburg PA
CBHW021129080526
44587CB00012B/1206